12 Critical Things

Your Family Needs to Know

by Mark Gavagan

This book is dedicated to my wonderful mother, Patricia

Published by Cole House LLC - Mendham, NJ USA

For inquiries about sales in bulk quantities, including corporate/premium sales, please contact the publisher at Cole House LLC P.O. Box 91 Mendham, NJ 07945 or the website www.12CriticalThings.com

Printed in the United States of America

About the Author:

Mark Gavagan is a Business/Economics graduate of Utica College and has a broad background in business and financial services. His career includes more than eighteen years as an equity trader, financial services registered representative, entrepreneur, writer, and Fortune 100 company manager.

His first book is "The It's All Right Here Life & Affairs Organizer"

Mark lives in northern New Jersey. He's married and has two daughters.

"My sincere thanks to Dave Martin, Colin Harris, Michael Connell and Patty-Lynn Connell for all of their insightful ideas and generous assistance." -Mark Gavagan

The Book's Title is "12 Critical Things..." Why So Many Pages?

Fair question. The title refers to the twelve major areas of critical decisions and information this book guides you to provide for your family.

Many of these twelve areas have multiple or even dozens of components. Also, some of the twelve major areas are written twice, so that each spouse may enter his or her own decisions and preferences.

Lastly, while this book totals approximately sixty pages including introductions and table of contents, it is based upon an extremely comprehensive 300-page publication titled "The It's All Right Here Life & Affairs Organizer"

What are the "12 Critical Things"?

I . **Personal & Family Info**

II . **Family Medical History**

III . **Insurance**

IV . **Investments, Bank Accounts & Other Financial Assets**

V . **Retirement Plans & Annuities**

VI . **Real Estate: Your Primary Residence**

VII . **Debts & Liabilities**

VIII . **Advisors**

IX . **Advance Health Care Directives**

X . **Organ Donation Choices**

XI . **Final Arrangements**

XII . **Wills, Trusts & Estate Plans**

*While often very difficult to think about and discuss, knowing what loved ones want can save time & money and be **very** comforting.*

Other important information is mixed into these pages that doesn't fit neatly into one of these categories, such as gifts of property, safe deposit box info, etc.

Contents

(continued on next page)

About This Book and How To Use It

The purpose of this book is to help you document your personal wishes and all the essential pieces of information your family would be likely to need in a crisis.

If you can't fit all of your items on a given page, enter the most important ones and summarize the others in the "Notes & Additional Info" section.

Time-Saving Temporary Shortcut - use a binder clips to attach a statement for each credit card, loan, lease, bank account, retirement plan, annuity, etc. to this book. These don't contain all the information a person might need, but they're a good start.

Copying Pages for Your Personal Use - you are welcome to copy any pages from this book for your own personal use. For example, you might want to have a duplicate of your medical history for when you go on vacation in case of an emergency.

Naming Beneficiaries for Assets - naming the right beneficiaries for your all of your assets is very important. While identifying the best choices can be complicated, the benefit is that you and your family can save substantial sums of money and possibly even avoid the costs and delays of probate court. Research the topic in books and articles, and consider consulting an experienced professional. Visit our website for books on this and other important topics.

Who Should You Notify About the Book's Contents and Location?

One or more friends, family members, and/or professional advisors who are responsible, trustworthy, and genuinely care about you.

Not everyone you notify about the this book's existence and the information it contains must have direct access to it.

Perhaps the most important thing is for the appropriate people to be aware of the book and, in the event of a crisis, who (including detailed contact information) can quickly access your decisions and information.

For example, a couple with five adult children might notify all of their offspring plus their lawyer and accountant, but give only one or two children who live locally copies of the combination or key to the water and fire protected safe their book is kept in.

While a criminal breaking into your home is probably seeking cash and valuables, it's important to keep this book and your personal information secure against theft.

Keeping Your Personal Information SECURE

Where Should You Store Your Book?

While security is important, so is making sure information and decisions you've taken the time to write down can be accessed when needed.

A bank safe deposit box probably isn't right because it can't be accessed when the bank is closed, or when any owner/lessor of a safe deposit box dies (depending upon the laws of your state).

For example, if a person were to suddenly die in an accident and this book were kept in a safe deposit box, it might be weeks or even months before it could be accessed to reveal important information that loved ones would need to know very quickly, such as decisions about organ donation and final arrangements.

Another concern is the loss of all information and decisions in the event of a flood, fire, or other natural disaster.

One of the best options to consider for storing this book that offers security from both identity theft and physical harm due to fire or flooding is a small water and fire resistant safe or lock box in a location that is hidden, yet accessible.

Be sure one or more people you notify about this book's location and contents know where your safe or lock box is and have the key or combination so they can access it quickly in a crisis.

Remember, in a crisis it must be reasonably easy for you or your loved ones to quickly access your information and decisions.

What Information Should You Include?

Think carefully about this. Just because there's a space for something, doesn't mean you should automatically write it down. The more secure your storage location, the more free you should feel to include sensitive information.

Like most things in life, the right decision depends upon applying common sense to your situation.

Symbol for Security-Sensitive Information

keep secure

We've placed this symbol near many spaces requesting information that you should be especially cautious about, from an identity theft standpoint.

It doesn't mean the requested information should never be entered - it means you should carefully consider how securely this book is stored when making your decisions.

There are many other instances where information you are prompted for may be sensitive from an identity theft standpoint, but there is no warning.

Use your best judgement and don't hesitate to seek professional advice.

Information About You

Full name	Maiden & other names
Address	**Email address & telephone number(s)**
Date & place of birth (city, county, state, country)	**Location of certified birth certificate**
Social Security number & card location ⚠️ **keep secure**	**Location of adoption papers, if applicable**
Driver's license number and state	**Location of religious documents**

Work / School

Occupation, title and name of institution	Your identification (ID) number(s)
Address, telephone # and website	**Contact person's name, email and telephone #**

Citizenship, Passport & Immigration

U.S. citizen? ☐ yes ☐ no Other countries of citizenship:

Passport <u>number</u>:   issued by:

  <u>storage location</u>:

U.S. Alien Registration number ('A' number or 'A#')	document location
U.S. Lawful Permanent Resident (LPR or I-551 or "Green Card")	document location

Information About You (cont'd)

Military Service and Records

Are you a veteran? ☐ yes ☐ no	If so, country and branch served

Induction date: ____ / ____ / _____
             mm   day   4 digit year
 	
Discharge date: ____ / ____ / _____
             mm   day   4 digit year
	Service I.D. number
	(this may or may not be your Social Security number)
	
	⚠ **keep secure**

Type of discharge received (honorable, etc.):	Rank at discharge
Location of discharge papers (DD-214)	Location of other military documents (specify)

Current Marriage

Spouse's current and maiden names	Date & place of marriage (city, county, state, country)
Location of marriage certificate	Location of prenuptial or postnuptial agreement, if any

Prior Marriage (if any prior to current)

Former spouse's current and maiden names	Date & place of marriage (city, county, state, country)
Location of marriage certificate	Location of prenuptial or postnuptial agreement, if any
Type, date & place of marriage termination ☐ divorce ☐ legal separation ☐ annulment ☐ death date: / / place:	Location of marriage termination documents
Active alimony or spousal support? ☐ yes ☐ no (if "yes", see that section for details & documents)	Active child support? ☐ yes ☐ no (if "yes", see that section for details & documents)

About Your Spouse or Partner

Full name	Maiden & other names
Address	**Email address & telephone number(s)**
Date & place of birth (city, county, state, country)	**Location of certified birth certificate**
Social Security number & card location ⚠️ **keep secure**	**Location of adoption papers, if applicable**
Driver's license number and state	**Location of religious documents**

Work / School

Occupation, title and name of institution	Your identification (ID) number(s)
Address, telephone # and website	**Contact person's name, email and telephone #**

Citizenship, Passport & Immigration

U.S. citizen? ☐ yes ☐ no   Other countries of citizenship:

Passport number: _____   issued by: _____

    storage location: _____

U.S. Alien Registration number ('A' number or 'A#')   document location

U.S. Lawful Permanent Resident (LPR or I-551 or "Green Card")   document location

About Your Spouse or Partner (cont'd)

Military Service and Records

Are you a veteran? □ yes □ no	If so, country and branch served

Induction date: ____ / ____ / _____
              mm   day   4 digit year
 	
Discharge date: ____ / ____ / _____
              mm   day   4 digit year
	Service I.D. number
	(this may or may not be your Social Security number)
	
	⚠️ **keep secure**

Type of discharge received (honorable, etc.):	Rank at discharge
Location of discharge papers (DD-214)	Location of other military documents (specify)

Prior Marriage (if any prior to current)

Former spouse's current and maiden names	Date & place of marriage (city, county, state, country)
Location of marriage certificate	Location of prenuptial or postnuptial agreement, if any

Type, date & place of marriage termination
    □ divorce   □ legal separation
    □ annulment □ death
 	
date: /   /   place:
	Location of marriage termination documents

Active alimony or spousal support? □ yes □ no (if "yes", enter details on later pages)	Active child support? □ yes □ no (if "yes", enter details on later pages)

Notes & Additional Info

Children, Grandchildren, Parents & Siblings

Name:_____ How related? _____

Date of birth:_____ Place of birth:_____

Address:_____

Phone number(s):_____

Email:_____ Alt. email: _____

Notes:

Name:_____ How related? _____

Date of birth:_____ Place of birth:_____

Address:_____

Phone number(s):_____

Email:_____ Alt. email: _____

Notes:

Name:_____ How related? _____

Date of birth:_____ Place of birth:_____

Address:_____

Phone number(s):_____

Email:_____ Alt. email: _____

Notes:

Name:_____ How related? _____

Date of birth:_____ Place of birth:_____

Address:_____

Phone number(s):_____

Email:_____ Alt. email: _____

Notes:

Children, Grandchildren, Parents & Siblings (cont'd)

Name:_____ How related? _____

Date of birth:_____ Place of birth:_____

Address:_____

Phone number(s):_____

Email:_____ Alt. email:_____

Notes:

Name:_____ How related? _____

Date of birth:_____ Place of birth:_____

Address:_____

Phone number(s):_____

Email:_____ Alt. email:_____

Notes:

Name:_____ How related? _____

Date of birth:_____ Place of birth:_____

Address:_____

Phone number(s):_____

Email:_____ Alt. email:_____

Notes:

Name:_____ How related? _____

Date of birth:_____ Place of birth:_____

Address:_____

Phone number(s):_____

Email:_____ Alt. email:_____

Notes:

Children, Grandchildren, Parents & Siblings (cont'd)

Name:_____ How related? _____

Date of birth:_____ Place of birth:_____

Address:_____

Phone number(s):_____

Email:_____ Alt. email:_____

Notes:

Name:_____ How related? _____

Date of birth:_____ Place of birth:_____

Address:_____

Phone number(s):_____

Email:_____ Alt. email:_____

Notes:

Name:_____ How related? _____

Date of birth:_____ Place of birth:_____

Address:_____

Phone number(s):_____

Email:_____ Alt. email:_____

Notes:

Name:_____ How related? _____

Date of birth:_____ Place of birth:_____

Address:_____

Phone number(s):_____

Email:_____ Alt. email:_____

Notes:

Children, Grandchildren, Parents & Siblings (cont'd)

Name:_____ How related? _____

Date of birth:_____ Place of birth:_____

Address:_____

Phone number(s):_____

Email:_____ Alt. email: _____

Notes:

Name:_____ How related? _____

Date of birth:_____ Place of birth:_____

Address:_____

Phone number(s):_____

Email:_____ Alt. email: _____

Notes:

Name:_____ How related? _____

Date of birth:_____ Place of birth:_____

Address:_____

Phone number(s):_____

Email:_____ Alt. email: _____

Notes:

Name:_____ How related? _____

Date of birth:_____ Place of birth:_____

Address:_____

Phone number(s):_____

Email:_____ Alt. email: _____

Notes:

Care or Support For Parents, Children, or Others

Care & Support Situation #1 - outline in detail* any care or support you and/or spouse provide (or expect to provide in the future) to one or more parents, siblings, or others. Think of "care or support" in broad terms, including any financial support, visitation, errands, transportation, etc.

_____
_____
_____
_____
_____
_____
_____
_____
_____
_____
_____
_____
_____
_____
_____

*Include names, schedules, dollar amounts, institutions, contact info, and arrangements you have made to provide this care or support in the event of a short-term emergency or your incapacity or death.

Care & Support Situation #2 - outline in detail any care or support you and/or spouse provide (or expect to provide in the future) to one or more parents, siblings, or others. Think of "care or support" in broad terms, including any financial support, visitation, errands, transportation, etc.

_____
_____
_____
_____
_____
_____
_____
_____
_____
_____
_____
_____

Alimony / Child Support

Alimony / Child Support #1

Type & Background: _____

_____

Who Owes? _____ Who Receives? _____

Payment Schedule $_____ per _____ End Date: _____ / _____
                                                                mm   4 digit year

Location of Documents: _____

Notes:

Alimony / Child Support #2

Type & Background: _____

_____

Who Owes? _____ Who Receives? _____

Payment Schedule $_____ per _____ End Date: _____ / _____
                                                                mm   4 digit year

Location of Documents: _____

Notes:

Alimony / Child Support #3

Type & Background: _____

_____

Who Owes? _____ Who Receives? _____

Payment Schedule $_____ per _____ End Date: _____ / _____
                                                                mm   4 digit year

Location of Documents: _____

Notes:

Alimony / Child Support #4

Type & Background: _____

_____

Who Owes? _____ Who Receives? _____

Payment Schedule $_____ per _____ End Date: _____ / _____
                                                                mm   4 digit year

Location of Documents: _____

Notes:

Your Medical History

Full name	Date of birth	Blood type
	____ / ____ / _____ mm day 4 digit year	

Prescription or Other Medications

Are you **currently taking any prescription or other medications?**   □ yes □ no

If yes, list each medication below and enter details (e.g. since when, specific reason for the medication, dosage, schedule of when taken, prescribing physician, etc.)

Your Medical History (cont'd)

Allergies

Are you allergic to any **drugs, medicines, foods, insect stings, etc.?**   □ yes □ no

If yes, list each allergy below along with its symptoms, treatment, how & when diagnosed, etc.

History of Surgeries & Procedures

Date & description	Details (include results, outlook, physician's name & location)

Your Medical History (cont'd)

Diseases, Illnesses, Symptoms & Medical Conditions

Item	Details (include dates, doctors, treatments, outlook, current status, etc.)

Your Medical History (cont'd)

Doctors & Other Health Care Providers (primary physician, specialists, pharmacist, dentist, etc)

Name, address & contact info	Type of care given

Spouse's Medical History

Full name	Date of birth	Blood type
	____ / ____ / _____ mm day 4 digit year	

Prescription or Other Medications

List any current **prescription or other medications** and details (e.g. reason for the medication, duration, dosage, schedule of when taken, prescribing physician, etc.):   ☐ none

Spouse's Medical History (cont'd)

Allergies

Are you allergic to any **drugs, medicines, foods, insect stings, etc.?**   ☐ yes ☐ no

If yes, list each allergy below along with its symptoms, treatment, how & when diagnosed, etc.

History of Surgeries & Procedures

Date & description	Details (include results, outlook, physician's name & location)

Spouse's Medical History (cont'd)

Diseases, Illnesses, Symptoms & Medical Conditions

Item	Details (include dates, doctors, treatments, outlook, current status, etc.)

Spouse's Medical History (cont'd)

Doctors & Other Health Care Providers (primary physician, specialists, pharmacist, dentist, etc)

Name, address & contact info	Type of care given

Extended Family's Medical History

Certain illnesses and diseases tend to run in families, including alcoholism, heart disease, high cholesterol, depression, diabetes, Alzheimer's, muscular dystrophy, and many types of cancer. These and others are believed to have genetic components that can pass from one generation to others.

Outline anything meaningful in your family's medical history below. Next, communicate this information to family members and physicians in order to instigate preventive measures and early diagnosis of symptoms.

Afflicted person's full name, date of birth, and relationship to you	Illness, disease or medical condition + details (include how and when diagnosed, treatments & results, contributing factors such as a tobacco smoker with lung cancer, and the names & locations of physicians)

Life Insurance

Life Insurance #1

Ins. Company:_____ Policy #:_____

Type:_____ Owner:_____

Whose Life is Insured?_____ Death Benefit $_____

Beneficiaries:_____

Location of Records:_____ Premiums:_____

Notes:

Life Insurance #2

Ins. Company:_____ Policy #:_____

Type:_____ Owner:_____

Whose Life is Insured?_____ Death Benefit $_____

Beneficiaries:_____

Location of Records:_____ Premiums:_____

Notes:

Life Insurance #3

Ins. Company:_____ Policy #:_____

Type:_____ Owner:_____

Whose Life is Insured?_____ Death Benefit $_____

Beneficiaries:_____

Location of Records:_____ Premiums:_____

Notes:

Life Insurance #4

Ins. Company:_____ Policy #:_____

Type:_____ Owner:_____

Whose Life is Insured?_____ Death Benefit $_____

Beneficiaries:_____

Location of Records:_____ Premiums:_____

Notes:

Policy #:_____

Owner:_____

_____

Premiums:_____

Policy #:_____

Owner:_____

Who Is Insured?_____

Benefits:_____

Location of Records:_____ Premiums:_____

Notes:

Health, Disability or LTC Insurance #3

Ins. Company:_____ Policy #:_____

Type:_____ Owner:_____

Who Is Insured?_____

Benefits:_____

Location of Records:_____ Premiums:_____

Notes:

Health, Disability or LTC Insurance #4

Ins. Company:_____ Policy #:_____

Type:_____ Owner:_____

Who Is Insured?_____

Benefits:_____

Location of Records:_____ Premiums:_____

Notes:

Bank Accounts

> Include certificates of deposit (CD's)

Bank Account #1

Firm's Name:_____ Account #:_____

Account Type:_____ Ownership Type:_____

Owners:_____

Beneficiaries:_____

Location of Records:_____ Value $_____ as of _____ / _____
                                                                    mm   4 digit year

Notes:

Bank Account #2

Firm's Name:_____ Account #:_____

Account Type:_____ Ownership Type:_____

Owners:_____

Beneficiaries:_____

Location of Records:_____ Value $_____ as of _____ / _____
                                                                    mm   4 digit year

Notes:

Bank Account #3

Firm's Name:_____ Account #:_____

Account Type:_____ Ownership Type:_____

Owners:_____

Beneficiaries:_____

Location of Records:_____ Value $_____ as of _____ / _____
                                                                    mm   4 digit year

Notes:

Bank Account #4

Firm's Name:_____ Account #:_____

Account Type:_____ Ownership Type:_____

Owners:_____

Beneficiaries:_____

Location of Records:_____ Value $_____ as of _____ / _____
                                                                    mm   4 digit year

Notes:

Bank Accounts (cont'd) > Include certificates of deposit (CD's)

Bank Account #5

Firm's Name:_____ Account #:_____

Account Type:_____ Ownership Type:_____

Owners:_____

Beneficiaries:_____

Location of Records:_____ Value $_____ as of _____ / _____
                                                                    mm   4 digit year

Notes:

Bank Account #6

Firm's Name:_____ Account #:_____

Account Type:_____ Ownership Type:_____

Owners:_____

Beneficiaries:_____

Location of Records:_____ Value $_____ as of _____ / _____
                                                                    mm   4 digit year

Notes:

Bank Account #7

Firm's Name:_____ Account #:_____

Account Type:_____ Ownership Type:_____

Owners:_____

Beneficiaries:_____

Location of Records:_____ Value $_____ as of _____ / _____
                                                                    mm   4 digit year

Notes:

Bank Account #8

Firm's Name:_____ Account #:_____

Account Type:_____ Ownership Type:_____

Owners:_____

Beneficiaries:_____

Location of Records:_____ Value $_____ as of _____ / _____
                                                                    mm   4 digit year

Notes:

Brokerage & Mutual Fund Accounts

Brokerage/ Mutual Fund Account #1

Firm's Name:_____ Account #:_____

Account Type:_____ Ownership Type:_____

Owners:_____

Beneficiaries:_____

Location of Records:_____ Value $_____ as of _____ /_____
                                                                    mm   4 digit year

Notes:

Brokerage/ Mutual Fund Account #2

Firm's Name:_____ Account #:_____

Account Type:_____ Ownership Type:_____

Owners:_____

Beneficiaries:_____

Location of Records:_____ Value $_____ as of _____ /_____
                                                                    mm   4 digit year

Notes:

Brokerage/ Mutual Fund Account #3

Firm's Name:_____ Account #:_____

Account Type:_____ Ownership Type:_____

Owners:_____

Beneficiaries:_____

Location of Records:_____ Value $_____ as of _____ /_____
                                                                    mm   4 digit year

Notes:

Brokerage/ Mutual Fund Account #4

Firm's Name:_____ Account #:_____

Account Type:_____ Ownership Type:_____

Owners:_____

Beneficiaries:_____

Location of Records:_____ Value $_____ as of _____ /_____
                                                                    mm   4 digit year

Notes:

Brokerage & Mutual Fund Accounts (cont'd)

Brokerage/ Mutual Fund Account #5

Firm's Name:_____ Account #:_____

Account Type:_____ Ownership Type:_____

Owners:_____

Beneficiaries:_____

Location of Records:_____ Value $_____ as of _____ / _____
 mm   4 digit year

Notes:

Brokerage/ Mutual Fund Account #6

Firm's Name:_____ Account #:_____

Account Type:_____ Ownership Type:_____

Owners:_____

Beneficiaries:_____

Location of Records:_____ Value $_____ as of _____ / _____
 mm   4 digit year

Notes:

Brokerage/ Mutual Fund Account #7

Firm's Name:_____ Account #:_____

Account Type:_____ Ownership Type:_____

Owners:_____

Beneficiaries:_____

Location of Records:_____ Value $_____ as of _____ / _____
 mm   4 digit year

Notes:

Brokerage/ Mutual Fund Account #8

Firm's Name:_____ Account #:_____

Account Type:_____ Ownership Type:_____

Owners:_____

Beneficiaries:_____

Location of Records:_____ Value $_____ as of _____ / _____
 mm   4 digit year

Notes:

Other Financial Assets	Including directly-owned stocks, savings bonds, municipal bonds, corporate bonds, privately held/restricted/unregistered stocks and other passive financial asset ownerships

Other Financial Asset #1

Name & description of this asset	Quantity of units owned (e.g. 500 shares)

	Estimated value: $	as of: _____ / _____ mm 4 digit year

Location of certificates/documents for this asset

Name of owner(s) & type* of ownership

Identification number(s) for this asset:

*How title is held - individual, joint tenancy, trust, etc

Notes*: _____

_____

_____

*Summarize this asset's purpose, time horizon, and investment strategy; describe in detail how and when this asset is to be sold or otherwise disposed of.

Other Financial Asset #2

Name & description of this asset	Quantity of units owned (e.g. 500 shares)

	Estimated value: $	as of: _____ / _____ mm 4 digit year

Location of certificates/documents for this asset

Name of owner(s) & type* of ownership

Identification number(s) for this asset:

*How title is held - individual, joint tenancy, trust, etc

Notes*: _____

_____

_____

*Summarize this asset's purpose, time horizon, and investment strategy; describe in detail how and when this asset is to be sold or otherwise disposed of.

Retirement Plans

Retirement Plan #1

Sponsor's Name:_____ Account #:_____

Plan Type:_____ Ownership Type:_____

Owners:_____

Beneficiaries:_____

Location of Records:_____ Value $_____ as of _____ / _____
                                                          mm   4 digit year

Notes:

Retirement Plan #2

Sponsor's Name:_____ Account #:_____

Plan Type:_____ Ownership Type:_____

Owners:_____

Beneficiaries:_____

Location of Records:_____ Value $_____ as of _____ / _____
                                                          mm   4 digit year

Notes:

Retirement Plan #3

Sponsor's Name:_____ Account #:_____

Plan Type:_____ Ownership Type:_____

Owners:_____

Beneficiaries:_____

Location of Records:_____ Value $_____ as of _____ / _____
                                                          mm   4 digit year

Notes:

Retirement Plan #4

Sponsor's Name:_____ Account #:_____

Plan Type:_____ Ownership Type:_____

Owners:_____

Beneficiaries:_____

Location of Records:_____ Value $_____ as of _____ / _____
                                                          mm   4 digit year

Notes:

Annuities

Annuity #1

Insurance Co.'s Name:_____

Account#:_____ Value $_____ as of _____ /_____
mm   4 digit year

Owners:_____

Annuitants (receive payout benefits):_____

Beneficiaries:_____

Date Annuity Was Purchased ("contract date"): _____ /_____ /_____
mm   day   4 digit year

Location of Records:_____

Annuity Payout Start Date (date payout benefits 1st received): _____ /_____ /_____
mm   day   4 digit year

Describe Payout Benefits:_____

Notes:_____

_____

Annuity #2

Insurance Co.'s Name:_____

Account#:_____ Value $_____ as of _____ /_____
mm   4 digit year

Owners:_____

Annuitants (receive payout benefits):_____

Beneficiaries:_____

Date Annuity Was Purchased ("contract date"): _____ /_____ /_____
mm   day   4 digit year

Location of Records:_____

Annuity Payout Start Date (date payout benefits 1st received): _____ /_____ /_____
mm   day   4 digit year

Describe Payout Benefits:_____

Notes:_____

_____

Real Estate: Primary Residence

Full Address (street, city, state, zip code, country)

_____

_____

_____

☐ check box if you/spouse own this location

Municipality (e.g. "Township of Morris")

County

Block number	Lot number

Purchase price:

$

Date of purchase

_____ / _____
mm   4 digit year

Estimated current value:

$

As of:

_____ / _____
mm   4 digit year

Annual property taxes:

$

As of:

_____ / _____
mm   4 digit year

Annual maintenance fees, association fees, etc:

$

As of:

_____ / _____
mm   4 digit year

Description*

_____

_____

_____

_____

*Type of property (single family house, condo, co-op, etc), number of bedrooms & bathrooms, lot size, etc

Liabilities* against this property (check all that apply)

☐ primary mortgage   ☐ secondary mortgage

☐ home equity loan(s)   ☐ home equity line of credit

☐ lien(s)   ☐ collateralization or securitization

☐ other: _____

*For detailed information, see the Loans & Leases section

Name of owner(s) & type* of ownership

_____

_____

_____

*Give details of exactly how title is held - individual, joint tenancy with right of survivorship, trust, community property, transfer-on-death deed, tenancy in common, etc

Location of capital improvement records & receipts

_____

_____

"Capital improvements" add to the value of your property or substantially prolong its life - these are different than repairs and maintenance, such as fixing a broken window. Capital improvements increase your cost basis in the property and may reduce taxes when the property is sold

Location of:

deed:_____

purchase documents:_____

title insurance:_____

other:_____

Notes: _____

_____

_____

_____

Real Estate: Primary Residence (cont'd)

Your Primary Residence (cont'd)

Description & location* of important keys needed for this property

key #1: _____

_____

key #2: _____

_____

key #3: _____

_____

key #4: _____

_____

key #5: _____

_____

*e.g. "Neighbor Dave Smith at 6 Maple has extra key for the front door - H: 555-555-0602   W: 555-555-0602"

Describe* how the items below operate or can be shut-off

alarm system: _____

_____

heating system: _____

_____

cooling system: _____

_____

main electrical service: _____

_____

gas supply: _____

_____

water supply: _____

_____

other: _____

_____

other: _____

_____

*Include any information someone new or unfamiliar with the property might need to know, such as the locations of switches, gauges, manuals & warranties, settings, operating tricks & quirks, etc.

Real Estate: Primary Residence (cont'd)

Service & Maintenance Providers (cont'd)

Type of Service	Company name, location & contact person	Telephone #, contact person & website	Summary of their past work & location of receipts/records
heating & air conditioning (HVAC) your account #:			
electrical your account #:			
plumbing your account #:			
alarm your account #:			
other (specify): your account #:			
other (specify): your account #:			
other (specify): your account #:			
other (specify): your account #:			

Inventory of Most Important Valuables

Item description & location	Value, date acquired & location of appraisal (if any)		
	current value $	as of ____ / ____ mm / 4 digit year	
	cost basis $	as of ____ / ____ mm / 4 digit year	
	location of original purchase documents		
	location of appraisal	☐ don't have one	
	current value $	as of ____ / ____ mm / 4 digit year	
	cost basis $	as of ____ / ____ mm / 4 digit year	
	location of original purchase documents		
	location of appraisal	☐ don't have one	
	current value $	as of ____ / ____ mm / 4 digit year	
	cost basis $	as of ____ / ____ mm / 4 digit year	
	location of original purchase documents		
	location of appraisal	☐ don't have one	
	current value $	as of ____ / ____ mm / 4 digit year	
	cost basis $	as of ____ / ____ mm / 4 digit year	
	location of original purchase documents		
	location of appraisal	☐ don't have one	

Tax Issues, Records & Strategies

Location of tax records	Who* has assisted in the preparation of your taxes?
	Give firm & person's name, address, telephone #, website and email. If a computer software program, give details including program name, manufacturer and version#

Notes: _____
_____
_____
_____

Do you/spouse have any ongoing or anticipated issue, audit, claim or dispute with any federal, state, local or other taxation body, such as the Internal Revenue Service? ☐ yes ☐ no	as of: ____ / _____ mm 4 digit year

If "yes", give details, including contact info for legal and other professional counsel:_____
_____
_____
_____
_____
_____
_____
_____
_____

Detail any tax planning, strategies, etc. your heirs, loved ones or advisors should be aware of in the event of your death or incapacity, including contact info for any legal or other professional counsel:
_____
_____
_____
_____
_____
_____
_____
_____
_____
_____
_____

Safe & Safe Deposit Box

Safe or Strongbox

Location of **safe** or strongbox ☐ don't have one	What is the safe combination or who has it (or the key) or where is it located? ⚠ **keep secure**
Notes + contents of your safe: _____ _____ _____ _____	

Safe Deposit Box

Location* of **safe deposit box** ☐ don't have one	Owner's name & date of birth
*Include company's name, telephone #, address & website	Name(s) & contact info for co-owner(s)
Location of safe deposit box key ⚠ **keep secure**	
Safe deposit box # or account #	Accessing a safe deposit box: Normally only the owner/ co-owner(s) have access. If owner is incapacitated, co-owners can still access, as can owner's agent under a durable power of attorney for finances, if any (see "Advance Health Care Directives" section for this info, including the location of these documents). ** Upon owner's death, state law will determine access **
Contents of safe deposit box: _____ _____ _____ _____	

Storage Unit - list storage unit contents in "Notes & Additional Info" at the end of this book

Location* of **storage unit** ☐ don't have one	What is the lock combination or who has it (or the key) or where is it located?
*Include company's name, telephone #, address & website	

Loan & Lease Obligations   > Include mortgages owed, car loans & leases, student loans, etc

Loan or Lease #1

Firm's Name:_____ Account #:_____

Type/Description:_____

Who Owes?_____ Location of Records:_____

Payment Schedule $_____ per _____ Interest Rate:_____

Balance $_____ as of ____ / _____ Date Loan/Lease Ends:____ / _____
                   mm   4 digit year   mm   4 digit year

Notes:

Loan or Lease #2

Firm's Name:_____ Account #:_____

Type/Description:_____

Who Owes?_____ Location of Records:_____

Payment Schedule $_____ per _____ Interest Rate:_____

Balance $_____ as of ____ / _____ Date Loan/Lease Ends:____ / _____
                   mm   4 digit year   mm   4 digit year

Notes:

Loan or Lease #3

Firm's Name:_____ Account #:_____

Type/Description:_____

Who Owes?_____ Location of Records:_____

Payment Schedule $_____ per _____ Interest Rate:_____

Balance $_____ as of ____ / _____ Date Loan/Lease Ends:____ / _____
                   mm   4 digit year   mm   4 digit year

Notes:

Loan or Lease #4

Firm's Name:_____ Account #:_____

Type/Description:_____

Who Owes?_____ Location of Records:_____

Payment Schedule $_____ per _____ Interest Rate:_____

Balance $_____ as of ____ / _____ Date Loan/Lease Ends:____ / _____
                   mm   4 digit year   mm   4 digit year

Notes:

Loan & Lease Obligations (cont'd)

Loan or Lease #5

Firm's Name:_____ Account #:_____

Type/Description:_____

Who Owes?_____ Location of Records:_____

Payment Schedule $_____ per _____ Interest Rate:_____

Balance $_____ as of ____/_____ Date Loan/Lease Ends:____/_____
                              mm   4 digit year   mm   4 digit year
Notes:

Loan or Lease #6

Firm's Name:_____ Account #:_____

Type/Description:_____

Who Owes?_____ Location of Records:_____

Payment Schedule $_____ per _____ Interest Rate:_____

Balance $_____ as of ____/_____ Date Loan/Lease Ends:____/_____
                              mm   4 digit year   mm   4 digit year
Notes:

Loan or Lease #7

Firm's Name:_____ Account #:_____

Type/Description:_____

Who Owes?_____ Location of Records:_____

Payment Schedule $_____ per _____ Interest Rate:_____

Balance $_____ as of ____/_____ Date Loan/Lease Ends:____/_____
                              mm   4 digit year   mm   4 digit year
Notes:

Loan or Lease #8

Firm's Name:_____ Account #:_____

Type/Description:_____

Who Owes?_____ Location of Records:_____

Payment Schedule $_____ per _____ Interest Rate:_____

Balance $_____ as of ____/_____ Date Loan/Lease Ends:____/_____
                              mm   4 digit year   mm   4 digit year
Notes:

Charge or Credit Cards

Credit or Charge Card #1

Firm's Name:_____ Account #:_____
(or last 4 digits)

⚠️ keep secure

Type/Description:_____

Who Owes?_____ Add'l Users:_____

Location of Records:_____

Balance $_____ as of ____ / _____ Interest Rate:_____ Annual Fee $_____
mm   4 digit year

Notes:

Credit or Charge Card #2

Firm's Name:_____ Account #:_____
(or last 4 digits)

Type/Description:_____

Who Owes?_____ Add'l Users:_____

Location of Records:_____

Balance $_____ as of ____ / _____ Interest Rate:_____ Annual Fee $_____
mm   4 digit year

Notes:

Credit or Charge Card #3

Firm's Name:_____ Account #:_____
(or last 4 digits)

Type/Description:_____

Who Owes?_____ Add'l Users:_____

Location of Records:_____

Balance $_____ as of ____ / _____ Interest Rate:_____ Annual Fee $_____
mm   4 digit year

Notes:

Credit or Charge Card #4

Firm's Name:_____ Account #:_____
(or last 4 digits)

Type/Description:_____

Who Owes?_____ Add'l Users:_____

Location of Records:_____

Balance $_____ as of ____ / _____ Interest Rate:_____ Annual Fee $_____
mm   4 digit year

Notes:

Charge or Credit Cards (cont'd)

Credit or Charge Card #5

Firm's Name:_____ Account #:_____
(or last 4 digits)

⚠ keep secure

Type/Description:_____

Who Owes?_____ Add'l Users:_____

Location of Records:_____

Balance $_____ as of ____/_____ Interest Rate:_____ Annual Fee $_____
mm   4 digit year

Notes:

Credit or Charge Card #6

Firm's Name:_____ Account #:_____
(or last 4 digits)

Type/Description:_____

Who Owes?_____ Add'l Users:_____

Location of Records:_____

Balance $_____ as of ____/_____ Interest Rate:_____ Annual Fee $_____
mm   4 digit year

Notes:

Credit or Charge Card #7

Firm's Name:_____ Account #:_____
(or last 4 digits)

Type/Description:_____

Who Owes?_____ Add'l Users:_____

Location of Records:_____

Balance $_____ as of ____/_____ Interest Rate:_____ Annual Fee $_____
mm   4 digit year

Notes:

Credit or Charge Card #8

Firm's Name:_____ Account #:_____
(or last 4 digits)

Type/Description:_____

Who Owes?_____ Add'l Users:_____

Location of Records:_____

Balance $_____ as of ____/_____ Interest Rate:_____ Annual Fee $_____
mm   4 digit year

Notes:

Advisors

> Such as your attorney, accountant, insurance or real estate agent, banker, clergy, architect, etc.

Advisor #1

Firm's Name:_____ Website:_____

Type of Advisor:_____

Contact Person:_____

Telephone #:_____ Email:_____

Location of Records:_____

Notes:

Advisor #2

Firm's Name:_____ Website:_____

Type of Advisor:_____

Contact Person:_____

Telephone #:_____ Email:_____

Location of Records:_____

Notes:

Advisor #3

Firm's Name:_____ Website:_____

Type of Advisor:_____

Contact Person:_____

Telephone #:_____ Email:_____

Location of Records:_____

Notes:

Advisor #4

Firm's Name:_____ Website:_____

Type of Advisor:_____

Contact Person:_____

Telephone #:_____ Email:_____

Location of Records:_____

Notes:

Advisors (cont'd)

Advisor #5

Firm's Name:_____ Website: _____

Type of Advisor:_____

Contact Person:_____

Telephone #:_____ Email:_____

Location of Records:_____

Notes:

Advisor #6

Firm's Name:_____ Website: _____

Type of Advisor:_____

Contact Person:_____

Telephone #:_____ Email:_____

Location of Records:_____

Notes:

Advisor #7

Firm's Name:_____ Website: _____

Type of Advisor:_____

Contact Person:_____

Telephone #:_____ Email:_____

Location of Records:_____

Notes:

Advisor #8

Firm's Name:_____ Website: _____

Type of Advisor:_____

Contact Person:_____

Telephone #:_____ Email:_____

Location of Records:_____

Notes:

Advance Health Care Directives

Your Advance Health Care Directives

Give details of each of your advance health care directive, including location of documents, where and when executed, and contact information for all agents, proxies, attorneys in fact, etc:

Spouse's Advance Health Care Directives

Give details of each of your advance health care directive, including location of documents, where and when executed, and contact information for all agents, proxies, attorneys in fact, etc:

Terms You Should Understand:

living will - a signed document directed towards health care professionals specifying the kind of care you wish to receive in the event that you become incapacitated and cannot communicate on your own behalf. This is also known as a "health care declaration" or "directive to physicians"

medical power of attorney - a signed document where you appoint a trusted person (your health care "agent" or "proxy" or "attorney in fact") to make medical decisions for you in the event that you become incapacitated and cannot communicate on your own behalf. This is also known as "durable power of attorney for health care"

financial power of attorney - a signed document where you appoint a trusted person (your financial "agent" or "proxy" or "attorney in fact") to pay bills, file insurance claims, and conduct other elements of your financial life.* This is also known as a durable power of attorney for finances

While "living will" and "medical power of attorney" are distinct from one another, some states combine these into a single document. A "financial power of attorney" is distinct from both, yet important.

All are *quickly & easily revocable* and can be written so that power(s) are granted to agents *only* in the event that your spouse becomes incapacitated and cannot communicate on his or her own behalf.

Organ Donation Choices

Be sure to discuss your organ & tissue decisions with loved ones so they can voice opinions & ask questions.

Donating organs & tissues when you die may save or enhance the lives of as many as 50 people.

There is no cost to you in donating. Open casket funerals can still take place afterwards, if that is your wish. No one is too old or too young, so don't rule yourself out as a potential donor. Even those with serious medical conditions often have many healthy and desperately needed organs and tissues to give.

>> While this page helps communicate your wishes to your loved ones, **each state has its own legal donor card form donors <u>must</u> sign** (and should carry) in order to be legally binding and ensure that your wishes are carried out. Also, make sure to fill-out donor forms on the back of driver's licenses.

To learn more, including information about how more than two dozen religions regard organ, tissue and whole body donation, and to access your state's specific donation documents, please visit a website run by the U.S. Dept. of Health and Human Services: www.OrganDonor.Gov or Donate Life America, a 501(c)(3) non-profit that links to each state's specific donation forms: www.DonateLife.Net or call (814) 782-4920

Your Donation Choices

Full name & signature	Date of birth
	____ / ____ / _____
	mm day 4 digit year

Upon my death, it is my desire to donate the following:

☐ Any needed organs or tissues (for transplant or the like into humans)

☐ Only the organs and tissues in the notes below (for transplant or the like into humans)

☐ My whole body to medical science (specify details below, including the receiving organization, instructions, location of documents, etc.)

☐ Nothing, I do NOT want to donate my organs, tissues or whole body

Notes*: _____

_____

*include the location of signed organ donor card/documents

Spouse's Donation Choices

Full name & signature	Date of birth
	____ / ____ / _____
	mm day 4 digit year

Upon my death, it is my desire to donate the following:

☐ Any needed organs or tissues (for transplant or the like into humans)

☐ Only the organs and tissues in the notes below (for transplant or the like into humans)

☐ My whole body to medical science (specify details below, including the receiving organization, instructions, location of documents, etc.)

☐ Nothing, I do NOT want to donate my organs, tissues or whole body

Notes*: _____

_____

*include the location of signed organ donor card/documents

The High Cost of Dying: Advice for Consumers

Excerpts from the nonprofit Funeral Consumers Alliance's publication "**Four-Step Funeral Planning: Where to Start When you Don't Know How to Start**":   (http://www.funerals.org/faq/fourstep.htm)

◆ A funeral can be simple or elaborate, inexpensive or costly. But unless you plan well in advance and shop around, you're likely to pay top dollar. Consumer surveys show that most people don't shop around for a funeral - they pick the funeral home closest to them, or the one their family has always used. Neither of these criteria tell you whether you're getting a good value. If you've never checked another funeral home for its prices and services, you may have been paying the highest rate in town for three generations.

◆ By federal regulation, funeral homes must give you price quotes over the phone. In addition, they must give you printed, itemized price lists when you show up in person to discuss funeral arrangements. That means you have the right to stop in to any funeral home and request a General Price List (GPL), no questions asked. It's a good idea to visit several funeral homes to pick up price lists and take them home for comparison at your own kitchen table. Share them with your family. Compare the cost of the items among funeral homes. You'll likely find a variation in price, sometimes quite substantial.

Excerpts from "**Funerals: A Consumer Guide**" by the U.S. Federal Trade Commission (FTC): published June, 2000 (available at http://www.ftc.gov/bcp/edu/pubs/consumer/products/pro19.shtm)

◆ When a loved one dies, grieving family members and friends often are confronted with dozens of decisions about the funeral - all of which must be made quickly and often under great emotional duress

◆ Funerals rank among the most expensive purchases many consumers will ever make. A traditional funeral, including a casket and vault, costs about $6,000, although "extras" like flowers, obituary notices, acknowledgment cards or limousines can add thousands of dollars to the bottom line. Many funerals run well over $10,000. [*Author's note: You can save thousands of dollars with good planning and comparison shopping*]

◆ Even if you're the kind of person who might haggle with a dozen dealers to get the best price on a new car, you're likely to feel uncomfortable comparing prices or negotiating over the details and cost of a funeral

◆ Some people "overspend" on a funeral or burial because they think of it as a reflection of their feelings for the deceased

◆ There's a federal law (The Funeral Rule) that makes it easier for you to choose only those goods and services you want or need and to pay only for those you select, whether you are making arrangements pre-need or at need

◆ The Funeral Rule, enforced by the Federal Trade Commission, requires funeral directors to give you itemized prices in person and, if you ask, over the phone. The Rule also requires funeral directors to give you other information about their goods and services. For example, if you ask about funeral arrangements in person, the funeral home must give you a written price list to keep that shows the goods and services the home offers. If you want to buy a casket or outer burial container, the funeral provider must show you descriptions of the available selections and the prices before actually showing you the caskets.

◆ Many funeral providers offer various "packages" of commonly selected goods and services that make up a funeral. But when you arrange for a funeral, you have the right to buy individual goods and services. That is, you do not have to accept a package that may include items you do not want.

◆ According to the Funeral Rule:

    - you have the right to choose the funeral goods and services you want (with some exceptions).

    - the funeral provider must state this right in writing on the general price list.

    - if state or local law requires you to buy any particular item, the funeral provider must disclose it on the price list, with a reference to the specific law.

    - the funeral provider may not refuse, or charge a fee, to handle a casket you bought elsewhere.

    - a funeral provider that offers cremations must make alternative containers available.

Your Final Arrangements	enter your name below

FIRST People to Contact Upon Your Death:

Name:_____ Relation:_____

Address:_____

Telephone#_____ Email:_____

Notes:

Name:_____ Relation:_____

Address:_____

Telephone#_____ Email:_____

Notes:

Budget Preferences

How costly should your overall final arrangements be?

   ☐ very inexpensive   ☐ low-to-moderate cost   ☐ higher-priced   ☐ premium

Notes:_____

Military Burial & Memorial Benefits

Are you eligible* for benefits from the U.S. Dept. of Veterans Affairs (VA)? ☐ yes ☐ no

Notes:_____

_____

*To learn more, visit the Dept. of Veterans Affairs website www.cem.va.gov or call 1-800-827-1000

Prearranged Funeral Plans / Memorial Society Membership

Do you have a prearranged funeral plan (some are legal contracts, while others are merely a record of wishes) ? ☐ yes ☐ no	If yes, is it "prepaid", meaning the customer paid money in advance ? ☐ yes ☐ no

Are you a member of any Memorial Society* ? ☐ yes ☐ no

*Memorial Societies (also known as Funeral or Cremation Organizations) are nonprofit consumer groups dedicated to protecting consumers' right to choose meaningful, dignified and affordable funerals.

To learn more, or to be referred to a nonsectarian, nonprofit, educational organization in your local area, visit the 501(c)(3) nonprofit Funeral Consumers Alliance at www.funerals.org or call (800) 765-0107

Notes*:_____

_____

_____

*Include location of documents and name, contact info, website & account number for each organization

Your Final Arrangements (cont'd)

Embalming

<u>Prior to cremation/burial, would you like to be embalmed*?</u>   □ yes   □ prefer no   □ definitely no

Notes: _____

*Embalming is the process of treating a dead body with chemical preservatives in order to temporarily prevent decay. It is rarely required by law and serves no public health purpose. "Eliminating this service can save you hundreds of dollars." (source: Federal Trade Commission). Green burial locations may restrict embalming due to the chemicals.

<u>Refrigeration is an inexpensive alternative</u> that serves the same purpose (even when there will be services where the body is present in an open casket). Some funeral homes don't have refrigeration facilities and thus may require embalming for viewing or visitation. Shop around.

Cremation

Would you like your body to be cremated?   □ yes   □ no   >> If "no" skip to next section

If yes, how soon after your death?

    □ right away*   □ after wake or viewing   □ after funeral or memorial services

*Immediate cremation, without embalming, is known as "direct cremation"

Do you have a pacemaker or any other implanted device, or have you received any radioactive medical treatments, such as Strontium-89 or Iodine-125 seeds? (the crematorium will need to know)

    □ yes   □ no   If yes, details:

Describe your preference for an urn or other receptacle* to hold your cremated remains:

    COST: □ very inexpensive   □ low-to-moderate cost   □ higher-priced   □ premium

Notes: _____

*It need not be an actual "urn" - you have a great deal of flexibility. Federal law prevents funeral providers from refusing to handle an urn or other cremains receptacle you acquire elsewhere or for charging a fee to do so.

Burial of Your Body or Cremated Remains

Would you like your body or cremated remains to be buried?

    □ yes, my **un**cremated body   □ yes, my cremated remains   □ no

If yes, how soon after your death?

    □ right away*   □ after wake or viewing   □ after funeral or memorial services

*Burial, performed shortly after death, without embalming, is known as "direct burial"

Eco-Friendly / Green Burial

Would you like to have an ecologically-friendly* ("green") burial?   □ yes   □ no

*The essence of a green burial is caring for a deceased person's body in an environmentally sensitive way, without the use of toxins and materials that are not biodegradable. For example, green burials do not use embalming (especially with formaldehyde), metal caskets, vaults or conventional markers.

For more information, visit (nonprofit) <u>Green Burial Counsel</u> at <u>www.greenburialcouncil.org</u> or (nonprofit) <u>Forest of Memories</u> at <u>www.forestofmemories.org</u>

Notes: _____

_____

Your Final Arrangements (cont'd)

Casket Preferences

What is your preference regarding the use of a <u>rental casket</u>* for wake and/or funeral services?

☐ do NOT want a rental casket   ☐ okay to use a rental casket   ☐ strongly prefer a rental casket

*Many consumers conserve natural resources and save a lot of money by <u>renting</u> a traditional casket (with a new removable insert liner) rather than purchasing one. Burial or cremation takes place using an inexpensive option like a simple pine box or a sturdy cardboard coffin.

If a viewing/funeral services casket will be purchased, how costly should it be?

☐ very inexpensive   ☐ low-to-moderate cost   ☐ higher-priced   ☐ premium

Notes:_____

_____

Gravestone, Headstone, Monument or Other Marker

Describe your preferences* regarding a marker at your gravesite, if applicable:

COST: ☐ very inexpensive   ☐ low-to-moderate cost   ☐ higher-priced   ☐ premium

Notes:_____

_____

_____

*Include preferences for inscription ("epitaph"), military/veteran, double or "companion" marker, design, etc.

Final Resting Place

What is the final resting place* for your body or cremated remains?

_____

_____

_____

_____

_____

* For example, "scatter cremated remains in the Pacific Ocean near Hawaii" or "Mausoleum space already purchased located at XYZ Cemetery in Queens, NY." Unless already noted in the "Prearranged Funeral Plans" section, include helpful details such as the location's address, telephone#, website, etc.

Preferred Charity for Memorial Donations

What charity or charities should memorial gifts in your name be donated to?

_____

_____

_____

☐ in lieu of flowers, make donations to the organization(s) above

Your Final Arrangements (cont'd)

Services

Indicate which services* (viewing, wake, visitation, funeral, memorial, etc.) you'd prefer and whether military/religious, body/cremains present, open/closed casket, music, hymns, prayers, speakers, etc.

_____

_____

_____

_____

_____

_____

*Learn more at **www.12CriticalThings.com**

Obituary

Would you like to have an obituary published?   ☐ yes ☐ no   With a photograph?   ☐ yes ☐ no

Details*:_____

_____

*Include the location/description of photo and/or pre-written text or summary of information to be used

Apparel & Jewelry

Describe below any clothing, jewelry, religious, or other items that should adorn or accompany your body or cremains at any time after your death

Item	Location	What should ultimately happen to the item?

Separate Funds for Final Expenses

Do you have funds designated for paying your final arrangements expenses?   ☐ yes ☐ no

Details*:_____

_____

_____

* Include the location of documents, account or policy #, institution's name, website & contact info, etc.

>> Ask your financial institution about "pay-on-death" options for these funds. Upon your death, the funds would be immediately available to the trusted person you name as beneficiary in order to carry-out your final arrangements

Spouse's Final Arrangements

enter name below

FIRST People to Contact Upon Your Death:

Name:_____ Relation:_____

Address:_____

Telephone#_____ Email:_____

Notes:

Name:_____ Relation:_____

Address:_____

Telephone#_____ Email:_____

Notes:

Budget Preferences

How costly should your overall final arrangements be?

☐ very inexpensive   ☐ low-to-moderate cost   ☐ higher-priced   ☐ premium

Notes:_____

Military Burial & Memorial Benefits

Are you eligible* for benefits from the U.S. Dept. of Veterans Affairs (VA)?   ☐ yes   ☐ no

Notes:_____

_____

*To learn more, visit the Dept. of Veterans Affairs website www.cem.va.gov or call 1-800-827-1000

Prearranged Funeral Plans / Memorial Society Membership

Do you have a prearranged funeral plan (some are legal contracts, while others are merely a record of wishes) ? ☐ yes ☐ no	If yes, is it "prepaid", meaning the customer paid money in advance ? ☐ yes ☐ no

Are you a member of any Memorial Society* ?   ☐ yes   ☐ no

*Memorial Societies (also known as Funeral or Cremation Organizations) are nonprofit consumer groups dedicated to protecting consumers' right to choose meaningful, dignified and affordable funerals.

To learn more, or to be referred to a nonsectarian, nonprofit, educational organization in your local area, visit the 501(c)(3) nonprofit Funeral Consumers Alliance at www.funerals.org or call (800) 765-0107

Notes*:_____

_____

_____

_____

*Include location of documents and name, contact info, website & account number for each organization

Spouse's Final Arrangements (cont'd)

Embalming

Prior to cremation/burial, would you like to be embalmed*? □ yes □ prefer no □ definitely no

Notes:_____

*Embalming is the process of treating a dead body with chemical preservatives in order to temporarily prevent decay. It is rarely required by law and serves no public health purpose. "Eliminating this service can save you hundreds of dollars." (source: Federal Trade Commission). Green burial locations may restrict embalming due to the chemicals.

Refrigeration is an inexpensive alternative that serves the same purpose (even when there will be services where the body is present in an open casket). Some funeral homes don't have refrigeration facilities and thus may require embalming for viewing or visitation. Shop around.

Cremation

Would you like your body to be cremated?   □ yes   □ no   >> If "no" skip to next section

If yes, how soon after your death?

□ right away*   □ after wake or viewing   □ after funeral or memorial services

*Immediate cremation, without embalming, is known as "direct cremation"

Do you have a pacemaker or any other implanted device, or have you received any radioactive medical treatments, such as Strontium-89 or Iodine-125 seeds? (the crematorium will need to know)

□ yes □ no   If yes, details:

Describe your preference for an urn or other receptacle* to hold your cremated remains:

COST: □ very inexpensive   □ low-to-moderate cost   □ higher-priced   □ premium

Notes:_____

*It need not be an actual "urn" - you have a great deal of flexibility. Federal law prevents funeral providers from refusing to handle an urn or other cremains receptacle you acquire elsewhere or for charging a fee to do so.

Burial of Your Body or Cremated Remains

Would you like your body or cremated remains to be buried?

□ yes, my uncremated body   □ yes, my cremated remains   □ no

If yes, how soon after your death?

□ right away*   □ after wake or viewing   □ after funeral or memorial services

*Burial, performed shortly after death, without embalming, is known as "direct burial"

Eco-Friendly / Green Burial

Would you like to have an ecologically-friendly* ("green") burial? □ yes □ no

*The essence of a green burial is caring for a deceased person's body in an environmentally sensitive way, without the use of toxins and materials that are not biodegradable. For example, green burials do not use embalming (especially with formaldehyde), metal caskets, vaults or conventional markers.

For more information, visit (nonprofit) Green Burial Counsel at www.greenburialcouncil.org or (nonprofit) Forest of Memories at www.forestofmemories.org

Notes:_____

_____

Spouse's Final Arrangements (cont'd)

Casket Preferences

What is your preference regarding the use of a <u>rental casket</u>* for wake and/or funeral services?

☐ do NOT want a rental casket   ☐ okay to use a rental casket   ☐ strongly prefer a rental casket

*Many consumers conserve natural resources and save a lot of money by <u>renting</u> a traditional casket (with a new removable insert liner) rather than purchasing one. Burial or cremation takes place using an inexpensive option like a simple pine box or a sturdy cardboard coffin.

If a viewing/funeral services casket will be purchased, how costly should it be?

☐ very inexpensive   ☐ low-to-moderate cost   ☐ higher-priced   ☐ premium

Notes:_____

_____

Gravestone, Headstone, Monument or Other Marker

Describe your preferences* regarding a marker at your gravesite, if applicable:

COST: ☐ very inexpensive   ☐ low-to-moderate cost   ☐ higher-priced   ☐ premium

Notes:_____

_____

_____

*Include preferences for inscription ("epitaph"), military/veteran, double or "companion" marker, design, etc.

Final Resting Place

What is the final resting place* for your body or cremated remains?

_____

_____

_____

_____

_____

* For example, "scatter cremated remains in the Pacific Ocean near Hawaii" or "Mausoleum space already purchased located at XYZ Cemetery in Queens, NY." Unless already noted in the "Prearranged Funeral Plans" section, include helpful details such as the location's address, telephone#, website, etc.

Preferred Charity for Memorial Donations

What charity or charities should memorial gifts in your name be donated to?

_____

_____

_____

☐ in lieu of flowers, make donations to the organization(s) above

Spouse's Final Arrangements (cont'd)

Services

Indicate which services* (viewing, wake, visitation, funeral, memorial, etc.) you'd prefer and whether military/religious, body/cremains present, open/closed casket, music, hymns, prayers, speakers, etc.

_____

_____

_____

_____

_____

_____

_____

_____

_____

*Learn more at **www.12CriticalThings.com**

Obituary

Would you like to have an obituary published?   ☐ yes ☐ no   With a photograph? ☐ yes ☐ no

Details*: _____

_____

*Include the location/description of photo and/or pre-written text or summary of information to be used

Apparel & Jewelry

Describe below any clothing, jewelry, religious, or other items that should adorn or accompany your body or cremains at any time after your death

Item	Location	What should ultimately happen to the item?

Separate Funds for Final Expenses

Do you have funds designated for paying your final arrangements expenses?   ☐ yes ☐ no

Details*: _____

_____

_____

* Include the location of documents, account or policy #, institution's name, website & contact info, etc.

>> Ask your financial institution about "pay-on-death" options for these funds. Upon your death, the funds would be immediately available to the trusted person you name as beneficiary in order to carry-out your final arrangements

Wills, Trusts & Estate Plans

Wills

A will (sometimes known as a "last will and testament") is the legal instrument that enables a person (the "testator") to make decisions on how, after death, his/her estate will be managed and distributed.

It is very important that you have a current and valid will. Otherwise:

(1) If you die without a valid will ("intestate"), the laws of the state you live in will determine such critical issues as who raises your children and what happens to your assets. Moreover, if you have no will when you die and you have no heirs in the eyes of your state's law (e.g. living children or parents), all of your assets may become the property of the state, instead of the friends, relatives or charities you would have chosen to inherit them; or

(2) If you die and have an out-of-date will, it may be declared invalid if it doesn't properly meet legal requirements (see "intestate" above); or

(3) If you die and have an out-of-date will that is valid, it will require that old decisions be carried out, even if they don't reflect your current wishes or circumstances. For example, you may end up leaving your entire estate to an ex-spouse instead of your favorite charity.

Do you have a will? ☐ yes ☐ no	If yes, when was it executed? ____ / ____ / _____ mm day 4 digit year	If yes, where (city, county & state) was it executed?
If yes, where is it located?	When and by whom was this will last reviewed? ____ / ____ / _____ mm day 4 digit year	

Method for creating this will and related information*
*If method = lawyer or other professional, note the full name, title, firm and contact information. If method = a "do-it-yourself" book or software program, full title, publisher and version#.

Below, list your estate's primary and alternate executors, as stated in your will.
(make sure they receive notification cards making them aware of this organizer's contents and location)

full name & address	phone # and alternate	email address
(primary)		
(alternate)		

Wills, Trusts & Estate Plans (cont'd)

Trusts

A "trust" is a type of legal entity, similar in some ways to a corporation or limited partnership, that holds legal title of ownership to assets for the benefit of one or more specified persons ("beneficiaries").

Trusts are often the primary tool in estate plans for controlling, managing and distributing assets in the manner specified by the person who created the trust (known as the trust's "Grantor"). Trusts are often established to direct what should happen with assets upon the death or incapacity of the "Grantor".

This is a complicated and evolving area of law - trusts should be created or reviewed (if using software, a paralegal or other like service) by an experienced attorney specializing in this field.

Describe any trusts, including exact legal name, formation date, purpose, & location of documents:

_____

_____

_____

_____

_____

_____

_____

_____

_____

_____

_____

_____

_____

_____

Trust Terminology:

<u>Grantor</u> - person who created the trust, also known as the trust's "Creator" or "Trustor" or "Settler"

<u>Trustee</u> - person or institution that administers the trust assets for the benefit of the beneficiaries

<u>Successor Trustee</u> - takes over administration of the trust in the event of the original Trustee's death or incapacity

<u>Beneficiary</u> - person or entity entitled to receive a trust's income or assets, per terms of the trust document

Estate Plans

An "estate plan" details the overall strategy for accomplishing estate planning objectives regarding how a person/family's assets & liabilities will be managed & distributed, especially after death.

Describe estate plans, if any, including where documents are located and contact info for advisors:

_____

_____

_____

_____

Gifts of Property *not otherwise specified in wills or trusts*

Sadly, many families are torn apart when grieving family members end-up fighting over family heirlooms, antiques, etc. The purpose of this section is to help your survivors avoid these emotional squabbles.

Specify below who gets what and under what circumstances (please specify). Remember, this is not a legal document and should not be expected to replace or supersede a will or trust. Seek advice from a qualified professional as needed.

Item's detailed description & location	To whom, when, and item's estimated value
	Who should this item go to?
	Under what circumstances? ☐ upon death of both "you" and "your spouse"
	Item's estimated value $ **as of** _____ / _____ mm 4 digit year
	Who should this item go to?
	Under what circumstances? ☐ upon death of both "you" and "your spouse"
	Item's estimated value $ **as of** _____ / _____ mm 4 digit year
	Who should this item go to?
	Under what circumstances? ☐ upon death of both "you" and "your spouse"
	Item's estimated value $ **as of** _____ / _____ mm 4 digit year
	Who should this item go to?
	Under what circumstances? ☐ upon death of both "you" and "your spouse"
	Item's estimated value $ **as of** _____ / _____ mm 4 digit year

Notes & Additional* Info:

* Examples: large personal loan or some other substantial obligation you owe or is owed to you; additional children or prior marriages, location of letters to loved ones to be opened upon your deaths, details about a pet's medication or special diet, etc.

Notes & Additional Info (cont'd)

Notes & Additional Info (cont'd)

Notes & Additional Info (cont'd)

ᴏʀᴅᴇʀ ꜰᴏʀᴍ - **FREE SHIPPING!**

(ᴀ ᴛᴇʀʀɪꜰɪᴄ <u>Gɪꜰᴛ</u> ᴛʜᴀᴛ <u>Eᴠᴇʀʏᴏɴᴇ</u> Nᴇᴇᴅs!)

12 Critical Things Your Family Needs to Know

THANK YOU. WE APPRECIATE YOUR BUSINESS.

Please write clearly. We will **not** share your personal information without your permission.

Buyer's Name _____

Address _____

City, State, Zip _____

Phone _____

Email _____

☐ Ship to the address above **(free)**

☐ Ship to one or more different addresses **(free)**
  (write each address on the back of this page)

Quantity Being Purchased _____

Total Amount $ _____

Prices Include _Free_ Shipping !

Single copy: $14.95

<u>Buy 2 or more and pay only $13.95 per</u>

2 copies - $27.90 (save $2.00)

3 copies - $41.85 (save $3.00)

4 copies - $55.80 (save $4.00)

5 copies - $69.75 (save $5.00)

>> For bulk and custom / private label
orders, contact us via our website
www.12CriticalThings.com

<u>Enclose check or money order* and **mail to**</u>:

Cole House LLC - 12 Critical Things Book Purchase
P.O. Box 91, Mendham, NJ 07945

prices include sales tax if we are obligated by law to collect

* Credit card purchases (with free shipping) and bulk orders at our secure website:

www.12CriticalThings.com

DIFFERENT OR MULTIPLE SHIPPING ADDRESSES

(INCLUDING GIFT PURCHASES)

Shipping Address #1   (please write very clearly)

To _____   How Many Books to this Address ? _____

Address _____

City _____ State _____ Zip _____

☐ DO NOT enclose a receipt   Gift From _____

Shipping Address #2

To _____   How Many Books to this Address ? _____

Address _____

City _____ State _____ Zip _____

☐ DO NOT enclose a receipt   Gift From _____

Shipping Address #3

To _____   How Many Books to this Address ? _____

Address _____

City _____ State _____ Zip _____

☐ DO NOT enclose a receipt   Gift From _____

Shipping Address #4

To _____   How Many Books to this Address ? _____

Address _____

City _____ State _____ Zip _____

☐ DO NOT enclose a receipt   Gift From _____

THANK YOU. WE APPRECIATE YOUR BUSINESS.

www.12CriticalThings.com

12 Critical Things Your Family Needs to Know